SACRED TEXTS

The
Tipitaka
and Buddhism

Anita Ganeri

A⁺

Smart Apple Media

Evans Brothers Limited
2A Portman Mansions
Chiltern St.
London W1U 6NR

First published 2003
Text copyright © Anita Ganeri 2003
© in the illustrations Evans Brothers Ltd 2003

Printed in Hong Kong by Wing King Tong Co. Ltd

Editors: Nicola Barber, Louise John
Designer: Simon Borrough
Illustrations: Tracy Fennell, Allied Artists
Production: Jenny Mulvanny
Consultant: Dr. Ulrich Pagel, School of Oriental and
African Studies, University of London

Picture acknowledgements:
Ancient Art and Architecture Collection Ltd: p9
bottom (Ronald Sheridan), p16.
theartarchive: p9 top (Dagli Orti), p18.
Circa Photo Library: p6 (Bipin J Mistry), p11, p13, p14
(William Holtby), p12, p17, p20 (William Holtby),
p22, p23 top (William Holtby), p25 (William Holtby),
p27 (William Holtby).
Hutchison Library: p7, p15 (P Goycolea), p23 bottom
(Michael Macintyre).
Trip: p21 (B Vikander), p24 (P Treanor).

Published in the United States by
Smart Apple Media, 1980 Lookout Drive,
North Mankato, Minnesota 56003

Library of Congress Cataloging-in-Publication Data

Ganeri, Anita, 1961–
The Tipitaka and Buddhism / Anita Ganeri.
p. cm. — (Sacred texts)
Summary: A discussion of Buddhism and some of its
sacred texts.
ISBN 1-58340-246-2
1. Buddhism—Sacred books—Juvenile literature.
[1. Buddhism. 2. Tripioaka.] I. Title. II. Sacred texts
(Mankato, Minn.)

BQ1138.G37 2003
294.3'82—dc21   2003042354

First Edition
9 8 7 6 5 4 3 2 1

In this book, dates are written using B.C.E., which means "before the common era," and C.E., which means "of the common era." These abbreviations replace B.C. ("before Christ") and A.D. (*anno domini*, "in the year of the Lord"), which are based on the Christian calendar.

The quotations in this book have been translated, and adapted to suit the age range, from the original text of the Pali Canon (Tipitaka) and other Buddhist texts. The book uses Pali spellings, except where the Sanskrit version is more usual (see the box on page 10 for more information about Pali and Sanskrit).

Contents

In each of the world's six main religions—Buddhism, Christianity, Hinduism, Islam, Judaism, and Sikhism—sacred texts play an important part. They teach people how to practice their faith and guide them through their lives. Wherever these books are read or studied, they are treated with great care and respect because they are so precious.

Introduction

Buddhist sacred texts

Buddhists follow the teachings of a man called Siddhattha Gotama, who lived in India about 2,500 years ago. Siddhattha Gotama became known as the Buddha, or the "enlightened one." Buddhists do not worship him as a god, but honor him as a very special human being who discovered the truth about the world. Buddhists use the Buddha's teachings as a guide for living better and happier lives. These teachings are known as the dhamma. They are found in the many hundreds of texts that make up the sacred texts of Buddhism.

How Buddhism began

Buddhism began in northern India in the fifth century B.C.E. Siddhattha Gotama was born in about 480 B.C.E., in Lumbini, which today lies in the neighboring country of Nepal. As the son of a wealthy ruler, he was raised in great luxury. Despite this, Siddhattha did not feel content. He was determined to discover why there was so much suffering in the world, and to teach people a way to overcome their sorrow and pain.

A Buddhist monk studying a sacred text. The texts contain the Buddha's teachings.

A Buddhist vihara (temple) in London, England.

The holy books

Unlike religions such as Christianity and Islam, Buddhism does not have just one sacred text. There are many different groups of Buddhists who follow their own sets of scriptures. Some texts are said to contain the teachings spoken by the Buddha. Others are the writings of great Buddhist teachers and monks. The two main groups of Buddhists are the Theravada and Mahayana schools. The sacred texts of the Theravada Buddhists are brought together in the Tipitaka, or Pali Canon. Mahayana Buddhists have their own sacred texts, called the Mahayana sutras.

Buddhism today

There are about 400 million Buddhists living all over the world. Most Buddhists still live in Asia, where Buddhism began. Today, most people in India are Hindus, but in some countries, such as Thailand and Sri Lanka, the majority of people are Buddhist. More recently, Buddhism has also become popular in Europe and North America.

> "Better than a thousand useless words is one single word that brings peace.
> Better than a thousand useless verses is one single verse that brings peace.
> Better than a hundred useless poems is one single poem that brings peace."
>
> (THE DHAMMAPADA, VERSES 100–102)

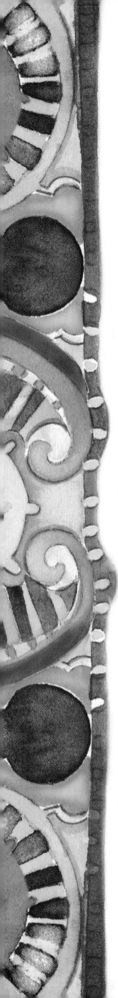

Origins

The life of the Buddha

The story of the Buddha's life is told in the Buddhist sacred texts. Most of what we know comes from the Tipitaka, together with later legends. According to the story, when Siddhattha was born, a wise man visited his father. The wise man predicted that Siddhattha would become a great king, or a great holy man. Wishing him to be a king, Siddhattha's father shielded his son from the outside world inside his splendid palace. In time, Siddhattha married his beautiful cousin and had a son, Rahula.

The four sights

One day, Siddhattha secretly left the palace, on a chariot ride. What he saw was to change his life. For the first time, he saw a frail old man, a sick man, and a corpse. Siddhattha had never seen people suffer like this. Then he saw a holy man who, despite having given up everything he owned, seemed content and happy. Siddhattha vowed to follow his example. That night, he left the palace to search for an answer to the problem of suffering.

Towards understanding

For six long years, the story says, Siddhattha lived in the forest with a group of holy men. Despite hunger and hardship, he did not find the answer for which he was searching. Then, one day, close to the

The first biography of the Buddha was written in the first century C.E. by an Indian poet called Ashvagosha. It was called the Buddhacarita, or "The Acts of the Buddha," and was written as a long poem. It gives the first full account of the Buddha's life, from his birth to his death.

village of Bodh Gaya, he sat down under a tree to meditate. There he gained enlightenment. Suddenly, he realized why people suffered and how their suffering could be stopped. From that time on, he became known as the Buddha, or the "enlightened one."

What the Buddha taught

The Buddha spent the rest of his life travelling around India and teaching people what he had learned. He and his followers lived as wandering monks. When he was 80 years old, the Buddha became ill and passed away. Before he died, he did not name a successor to carry on his work after he had gone. Instead, he told his followers not to be sad, but to use his teachings as a light to guide them. Legend says that an earthquake shook the ground when the Buddha died, just as it did at his birth and enlightenment.

The Buddha preaching his first sermon.

A scene showing the Buddha's death.

"When I am gone, do not say that you have no teacher. Whatever I have taught you, let that be your teacher when I am gone."

(Mahaparinibbana Sutta: Pali Canon)

Collecting the sacred texts

For centuries after the Buddha's death, his teachings were memorized by Buddhist monks and passed on by word of mouth. They were recited at festivals and other special occasions. It was not until the first century B.C.E. that the teachings were finally written down in the ancient Indian language of Pali. These texts were brought together as the Tipitaka (Pali Canon) and became the sacred texts of the Theravada Buddhists.

The first sacred texts of Buddhism were written down in Pali, a language similar to the one that the Buddha is thought to have spoken. Later texts were written in Sanskrit, another ancient Indian language. This is why there are often two spellings for Buddhist words. For example, in Pali, the word for the Buddha's teachings is "dhamma"; in Sanskrit, it is "dharma." The Sanskrit word "sutra" is spelled "sutta" in Pali.

"Go forth, O monks, for the good of the many, for the welfare of the many. Out of compassion for the world teach this dhamma, which is glorious in the beginning, glorious in the middle, and glorious at the end, in the spirit and in the letter."

(VINAYA PITAKA: PALI CANON)

Collecting the sacred texts

When the Buddha died, the monks worried that his teachings would be lost. Tradition says that 500 senior monks met to collect the Buddha's teachings and to agree on a final version. The Buddha's closest companion, Ananda, recited the dhamma, while another monk recited rules for monks and nuns.

The great split

About a hundred years after this first meeting, another gathering of monks was held to look at the teachings again. At this second meeting, different opinions arose about how the rules for monks and nuns should be kept. Some time later, Buddhism split into two main groups—Theravada, or "way of the elders," and Mahayana, or "great vehicle." Both groups follow the same basic teachings, but they have different ways of looking at them. Theravada Buddhism spread south to Sri Lanka, Myanmar, Thailand, Cambodia, and Laos. Mahayana Buddhism spread northwest to Nepal, Tibet, Japan, China, Korea, and Vietnam.

Writing the texts down

At first, the monks learned the Buddha's teachings by heart and passed them on from teacher to pupil. Groups of monks regularly recited the teachings to help remember them. But in the first century B.C.E., the number of monks in Sri Lanka fell, and there were fewer monks left to memorize the teachings. The monks decided to write the teachings down before they were forgotten. These writings became the Pali Canon.

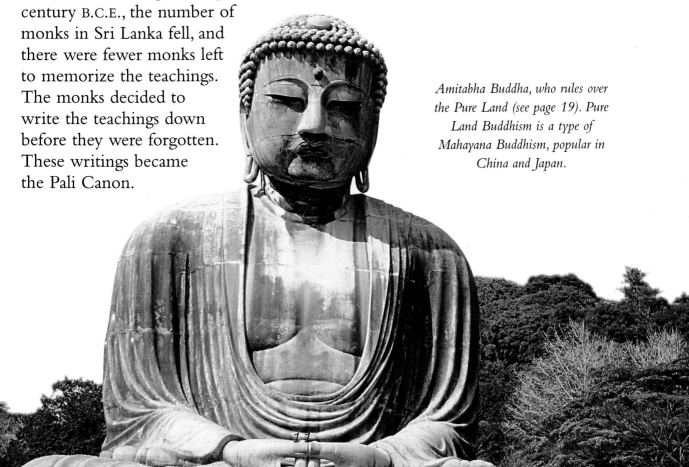

Amitabha Buddha, who rules over the Pure Land (see page 19). Pure Land Buddhism is a type of Mahayana Buddhism, popular in China and Japan.

Texts and Teachings

The Pali Canon

The Pali Canon is a set of texts which are sacred to the Theravada Buddhists. It is also called the Tipitaka (meaning "three baskets") because it was first written down on pages made from dried palm leaves, which were stored in three woven baskets. Each basket contained a different collection of teachings and writings.

Vinaya Pitaka

The first basket is called the Vinaya Pitaka. It sets out the 227 rules, given by the Buddha, about how Buddhist monks and nuns should live and behave. It also gives the reasons why the rules were made, and the penalties for breaking the rules. You can read more about the lives of Buddhist monks and nuns on pages 22 and 23.

A monk collecting gifts from local Buddhists in Myanmar. Monks rely on donations for everything they need.

Sutta Pitaka

The second basket is the Sutta Pitaka. It contains many discourses, or talks, by the Buddha which set out the key Buddhist teachings. These include the Four Noble Truths and the Noble Eightfold Path. In the Four Noble Truths, the Buddha taught that life is full of dukkha, which means unhappiness or suffering. The reason for this is that people are never content with what they have. They always want more. However, according to the Buddha's teachings, there is a way to end dukkha: people should live their lives according to the Noble Eightfold Path.

The Noble Eightfold Path

1. Right understanding—of the Buddha's teachings
2. Right thought—thinking good, kind thoughts
3. Right speech—speaking kindly; not telling lies
4. Right action—not killing or stealing; caring for others
5. Right livelihood—doing a job that does not harm others
6. Right effort—working hard to do good
7. Right mindfulness—thinking before you speak or act
8. Right concentration—training your mind to be calm by meditation

The eight-spoked dhamma wheel. Each spoke stands for a step on the Noble Eightfold Path.

The Buddha taught that life is like a wheel, turning in an endless circle of birth, death, and rebirth. What one's next life will be like depends on how he or she acts in this one. The only way to stop the wheel is to follow the Buddha's teachings. Then a person can gain enlightenment and reach nirvana, a state of perfect peace and happiness.

"There is a sphere which is neither earth, nor water, nor fire, nor air... which is neither this world nor the other world, neither sun nor moon. I deny that it is coming or going, enduring, death or birth. It is only the end of suffering."

(SUTTA PITAKA: PALI CANON)

Abhidhamma Pitaka

The third basket is the Abhidhamma Pitaka, which means "basket of higher teaching." It does not contain the words of the Buddha, but it includes commentaries and writings that help to explain the Buddha's teachings.

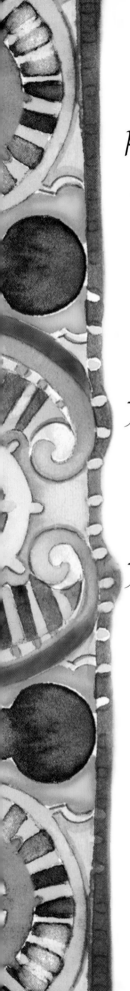

Popular texts

Ordinary Buddhists do not usually read texts from the Tipitaka. It is only monks and nuns who study most of these sacred texts and then explain their teachings. However, two parts of the Tipitaka are very popular and widely read. They are called the Dhammapada and the Jatakas. Buddhists treasure these texts and try to live by them.

The Dhammapada

The most famous section of the Tipitaka is part of the Sutta Pitaka, called the Dhammapada. This is a collection of the Buddha's sayings, in 423 verses. It sums up the dhamma, and offers guidance and advice for people seeking enlightenment.

An illustration from a Jataka story from Myanmar.

The Jatakas

The Jatakas also appear in the Sutta Pitaka. They are a collection of 547 stories about the Buddha's past lives, when he was often born as an animal. The stories teach important Buddhist values, such as friendship, compassion, wisdom, and generosity. The Buddha sometimes used stories to get his message across and to make it easier for people to understand the dhamma.

An illustration from a Jataka story painted on the wall of the Ajanta caves in India.

"Do not what is evil.
Do what is good.
Keep your mind pure.
This is the teaching
of the Buddha."

(THE DHAMMAPADA, VERSE 183)

The obedient elephant

In this Jataka story, the Buddha appears as an elephant to show that jealousy does not pay.

Once, there was a beautiful white elephant that belonged to the king. When the king rode the elephant through the streets, the crowds cheered for the elephant, not for the king. The king grew very jealous and wished the elephant dead. He told the elephant's rider to take it to the top of a high mountain. Then he ordered the beast to stand on three legs, then on its two back legs, then its two front legs, hoping that it would fall. Each time, the elephant obeyed. Then the king ordered it to stand in mid-air. The elephant obeyed. Not only did it stand in mid-air, but it flew far away, to the palace of another king. This king was so happy to receive the elephant that he split his kingdom into three parts, one for himself, and one each for the elephant and its rider. And as a reward for his fairness and kindness, his power grew until he ruled over all of India.

Mahayana scriptures

Mahayana Buddhists have their own set of sacred texts, called sutras (in Pali: suttas). The word "sutra" means a "string" or "thread." In Buddhism, it is used to refer to a short piece of teaching which is easy to understand. The earliest Mahayana scriptures were written down in the ancient Indian language of Sanskrit, in the first century C.E. They were later translated into other languages, such as Chinese, Tibetan, and Japanese.

The Buddha preaching the Lotus Sutra to his followers.

The Lotus Sutra

One of the most important Mahayana texts is called the Lotus Sutra. Mahayana Buddhists treat this sutra with great honor and respect. It is particularly popular in China and Japan. A long volume of verses and stories, it is the text of a talk given by the Buddha to a huge audience of followers and bodhisattvas (see right) at a place called Vulture Peak, near the city of Rajagriha in northern India.

Teachings of the Lotus Sutra

The Lotus Sutra contains many important Mahayana teachings. One is the belief that everyone, not just holy

16

men and women, can become a Buddha. Another is the belief in godlike beings, called bodhisattvas. Bodhisattvas are people who have gained enlightenment, and so could enter nirvana. Instead, they choose to stay in the world to help others become enlightened. Mahayana Buddhists pray to the bodhisattvas to help them gain enlightenment and overcome problems in their daily lives.

Kuan-yin, the bodhisattva of compassion.

"Suppose there were ten thousand living beings who, seeking for silver and gold, set out on the great sea. And suppose a fierce wind blew their ship to the land of the demons. If just one of them calls the name of Avalokitesvara, they will all be saved."

(THE LOTUS SUTRA)

Bodhisattvas

In Mahayana Buddhism, there are many bodhisattvas. Chapter 25 of the Lotus Sutra is all about one of the most popular bodhisattvas of all, called Avalokitesvara. He is worshipped for his great compassion and willingness to help anyone in trouble. In China, Avalokitesvara is called Kuan-yin; in Japan, he is known as Kannon.

Lotus flowers are very important symbols for Buddhists. They stand for goodness and purity. They show how people can rise above the sufferings of life to reach enlightenment, just as the lotus flowers rise above muddy water to bloom.

More Mahayana scriptures

In addition to the Lotus Sutra (see page 16), there are many other sutras that are important to Mahayana Buddhists. New texts were written as Buddhism spread beyond India. These sutras often mixed myths and legends with historical facts and events.

A page from the Diamond Sutra.

Perfect Wisdom

The Heart Sutra and the Diamond Sutra are two famous sutras which belong to a set of texts called the sutras of Perfect Wisdom. It is said that they were the words of the Buddha, but were too difficult for his followers to understand. They were stored in the Palace of the Nagas (serpent-kings) and later revealed to a great Buddhist teacher who brought them to this world. They teach about Perfect Wisdom, or seeing the truth about things. This means realizing that nothing is lasting or fixed. Everything is made up of elements that are constantly changing.

Translating the sacred texts

As Buddhism spread, Chinese monks made long journeys to India to visit the holy sites of Buddhism and to collect copies of the sacred texts. They took these texts back to China for translation. In the seventh century C.E., a monk called Hsuan Tsang is said to have brought back more than 500 texts, using 20 horses to carry them all.

Two sutras, written in the second century C.E., describe a beautiful, heavenly land, called the Pure Land. It is ruled over by Amitabha Buddha. Mahayana Buddhists who have faith in Amitabha, and chant his name, hope to be reborn in the Pure Land and move closer to nirvana. Pure Land Buddhism is especially popular in China and Japan (see page 11).

"This Pure Land is rich and prosperous, comfortable, fertile, delightful, and crowded with many gods and men. There are no hells, no animals, and no ghosts. It is rich in fruit and flowers, and decorated with jewelled trees."

(PURE LAND SUTRA)

Printing copies of the sacred texts

At first, the sutras were copied out by hand, but this was a long and difficult job for the monks. In about the eighth century C.E., the Chinese invented block printing, using wooden blocks dipped in ink to print words and pages. The oldest printed book in the world is a copy of the Diamond Sutra, dating from the ninth century C.E. Printing meant that many more copies of the texts could be easily produced and circulated.

Tibetan sacred texts

In the seventh century C.E., Buddhism travelled from India to Tibet, where it became the main religion. Tibetans follow a type of Mahayana Buddhism called Tantrayana, which mixes Mahayana and Tantric beliefs. Tantric Buddhism uses magic and rituals to help people gain enlightenment more quickly. It gets its name from a collection of mysterious sacred texts called the Tantras.

Tibetan Buddhists chant sacred words, called mantras, to help them clear their minds for meditation and to express their wishes to the bodhisattvas. The most famous mantra is "Om mani padme hum," which means "Hail to the jewel in the lotus." Mantras are written on prayer wheels, stones, and cloth. Spinning a prayer wheel is believed to release the mantra into the world and activate its cleansing power.

The mantra "Om mani padme hum," painted on stones in Tibet.

Kanjur and Tenjur

The sacred texts of the Tibetan Buddhists are divided into two large collections, called the Kanjur and the Tenjur. The Kanjur means "Translated Word of the Buddha." It is made up of 108 volumes that contain more than 1,000 texts of the Buddha's teachings. The Tenjur means "Treatises." It is made up of 225 volumes that contain more than 3,000 commentaries on the texts found in the Kanjur, together with poems and hymns of praise. Both of these collections are translations of Indian Buddhist writings.

The Tibetan Book of the Dead

The Bardo Thodrol, or Tibetan Book of the Dead, is a famous Tibetan scripture. It deals with death, life after death, and rebirth. According to the book, a world called Bardo lies between death and rebirth. When a person is dying, a monk reads passages from the Bardo Thodrol to him or her, to explain what is happening. The words are also intended to guide the person safely through Bardo, and the time between one life and the next.

A young monk spinning giant prayer wheels in a monastery in Tibet.

"Everything I see and hear is a teacher that teaches me the path to follow. The flowing of the water teaches me that nothing lasts forever... I do not need books made of paper and ink. Everything I see around me teaches me the dharma."

(THE SONGS OF MILAREPA)

Milarepa's songs

Milarepa was a great Buddhist saint and poet who lived in Tibet from 1043 to 1123 C.E. He left behind a collection of beautiful religious songs, called "The Hundred Thousand Songs of Milarepa." These songs are a popular part of the Tibetan Buddhist scriptures and are traditionally sung in homes as families go about their everyday lives and work.

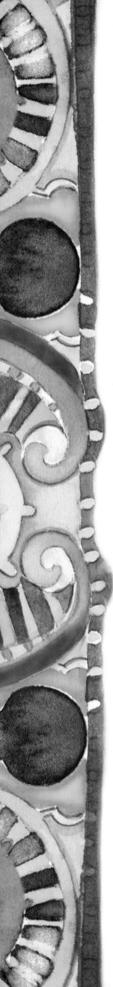

Study and Reading

Monks and libraries

After his enlightenment, the Buddha lived as a monk. Many of his followers copied his example. They travelled throughout India, teaching the dhamma. The monks and nuns did not have many belongings and relied on donations for their food and other everyday needs. Today, Buddhist monks dedicate their lives to practicing and teaching the Buddha's message.

Vinaya Pitaka

Buddhist monks and nuns live strict, simple lives, according to a set of rules called the vinaya, or monastic code. In Theravada Buddhism, these rules are found in the Vinaya Pitaka of the Pali Canon. There are 227 rules that set out how monks should live and behave, how the sangha (Buddhist community) should be organized, and the nature of the monks' duties. Every two weeks, the monks meet to recite the rules. Anyone who breaks a rule is expected to own up. There is also a similar but stricter section of rules for nuns.

A group of monks studying the sacred texts in a Tibetan monastery in Britain.

"Eat the alms placed in the bowl.
Do not ask for more food.
Do not be envious of what others are eating.
Do not talk with food in the mouth.
Do not smack the lips while eating."

(VINAYA PITAKA: PALI CANON)

Study and meditation

Buddhist monks and nuns spend most of their time in study and meditation. They read and chant from the sacred texts, and teach people about them. Many monks learn large parts of the texts by heart. Monks and nuns also observe Ten Moral Precepts, or commitments. These include caring for other living things, not stealing, not lying, and not eating after midday.

Monks meditating in Thailand.

Earning merit

The monks who translated and copied the sacred texts were greatly honored and respected. In Tibetan monasteries, books were traditionally made with long, rectangular pages, copying the shape of the original palm leaves from India. The pages were covered in silk and bound between wooden covers. This is still done today. In the past, Tibetan monasteries had huge libraries of books, but very few now remain.

Traditionally, Buddhist monks and nuns are allowed to own only eight items: robes, a belt, a needle and thread, a razor, an alms bowl, a walking stick, a water strainer, and a toothpick. These rules were laid down in the Vinaya.

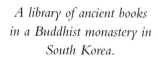

A library of ancient books in a Buddhist monastery in South Korea.

In Daily Life

Daily practice

Buddhists try to live their lives according to the Buddha's teachings, which are set out in the sacred texts. Studying and chanting from the texts is an important form of Buddhist practice. Ordinary Buddhists very rarely read the texts themselves because very few can understand Pali, Sanskrit, or the other languages in which the texts are written. It is left to the monks to explain the meaning of the texts and to teach people the words to chant.

Showing respect

Some Buddhists go to the vihara, or monastery, to honor the Buddha. They also practice their religion at home. When Buddhists visit a vihara, they go into the shrine room. There, they kneel or sit in front of an image of the Buddha. This is called puja. The devotees place offerings of flowers, candles, and incense in front of the Buddha. They repeat the Five Moral Precepts (a shorter version of the Ten Moral Precepts; see page 23) and pledge their commitment to the Three Jewels (see page 25). They may also spend time listening to the monks chanting from the sacred texts.

A Buddhist placing an offering of candles in front of an image of the Buddha, in Thailand.

The Three Jewels

The Three Jewels of Buddhism are the Buddha, the dhamma (the Buddha's teachings), and the sangha (the Buddhist community). Buddhists call them "jewels" or "treasures" because they are so precious. Buddhists show their commitment to the Three Jewels by reciting these words from the Sutta Pitaka, in the Tipitaka.

"I go to the Buddha as my refuge.
I go to the Dhamma as my refuge.
I go to the Sangha as my refuge."

The sacred texts give advice on many aspects of daily life. In part of the Sutta Pitaka, called the Digha Nikaya, the Buddha explained the importance of family duties. These included looking after one's parents, obeying one's teachers, and being helpful and loyal to one's friends.

A monk leading Buddhists in puja in a temple in Myanmar.

The Metta Sutta

The Metta Sutta is a famous talk given by the Buddha. It is found in the Sutta Pitaka of the Tipitaka. It teaches the importance of metta, or loving kindness, one of the highest qualities a Buddhist can have. Many Buddhists recite this sutta daily, or as part of puja. Part of the Metta Sutta appears on the right.

"May all beings be happy!
May their hearts be whole!
Whatever beings they are—
Those who are weak or strong,
Tall, short, or medium,
Small or large,
Beings seen or unseen,
Those who live near or far away,
Those who are born,
And those who are yet to be born.
May all beings be happy!"

(THE METTA SUTTA)

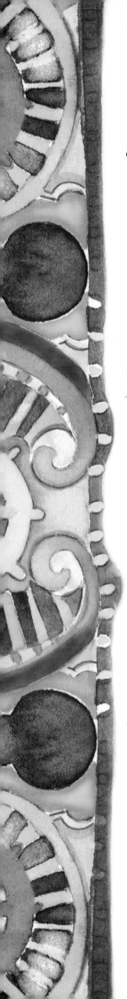

Special occasions

Throughout the year, there are many Buddhist festivals and celebrations. They mark events in the Buddha's life, points of his teaching, or key times in people's lives. These occasions often include talks and chanting from the sacred texts, performed by the monks. In Tibet and other countries, the texts are usually placed on an altar in front of the shrine.

Texts and blessings

Theravada Buddhists believe that some sacred texts have the power to protect them from harm. They listen to the monks chanting these special verses, which are called pirit. A pirit ceremony may be held when a person is ill or troubled, or on special occasions, such as getting married or moving to a new house. The verses often come from the Metta Sutta (see page 25) or the Ratana Sutta. Both are part of the Sutta Pitaka, in the Tipitaka.

The Ratana Sutta was another talk given by the Buddha. The word "ratana" means "jewel." In this talk, the Buddha teaches his listeners about showing loving kindness to others and praises the Three Jewels (see page 25). After each Jewel is discussed, the following words are repeated:

"This rare Jewel is in the Enlightened One;

By this truth may there be well being."

Festival tales

Some Buddhist festivals are celebrated by all Buddhists around the world. Others are special to a particular country. For example, the festival of Loi Kratong is a festival of light, held in Thailand in November. People float lighted candles on the rivers to carry bad luck away. They also listen to a famous Jataka story (see page 14), which tells of the time when the Buddha was reborn as Prince Vessantara. He was so generous that he gave his wife and children away.

Death

In the sacred texts, the Buddha teaches that nothing lasts forever. Everything is constantly changing. Buddhists try to remember this when someone dies, because dying is part of that change. At the funeral service, the monks chant from the sacred texts about this teaching.

As part of the service, the family sits together and pours water into a cup until it overflows. This is said to carry good deeds to the dead person for a higher rebirth. While they do this, the monks chant the verses below.

The funeral procession of a senior monk in Thailand.

"Just as water which falls on high ground
Flows to a lower level,
Even so, what is given here
Goes to the departed.

Just as mighty rivers
Flow into the great ocean,
Even so, what is given here
Goes to the departed."

(KHUDDAKAPATHA, PALI CANON)

glossary

Abhidhamma Pitaka The third of the three collections of texts which make up the Pali Canon. These texts help to explain the Buddha's teachings.

Bardo According to Tibetan Buddhist beliefs, a world that lies between the worlds of death and rebirth.

Bardo Thodrol A famous Tibetan sacred text that deals with death, the afterlife, and rebirth. It is also called the Tibetan Book of the Dead.

Bodhisattva A godlike being, worshipped by Mahayana Buddhists, who puts off enlightenment in order to help other people.

Buddha The title given to Siddhattha Gotama after his enlightenment. It means "awakened one" or "enlightened one."

Commentary A text that comments on, discusses, or explains another text or book.

Dhamma The teachings of the Buddha (in Sanskrit: dharma).

Dhammapada A collection of the Buddha's sayings which forms part of the Pali Canon.

Diamond Sutra A very important Mahayana sutra which teaches about Perfect Wisdom. This sutra is thought to have the power to cut through ignorance, like a diamond.

Dukkha Suffering, or being unhappy or dissatisfied.

Enlightenment The experience of understanding the truth.

Four Noble Truths One of the key teachings of Buddhism. The Four Noble Truths set out the reasons why people suffer, and show a way out of this suffering.

Heart Sutra A very important Mahayana sutra which teaches about Perfect Wisdom.

Jatakas Stories about the Buddha's past lives that appear in the Pali Canon.

Kanjur One of the collections of sacred texts of the Tibetan Buddhists.

Lotus Sutra One of the most important Mahayana sutras. It contains many teachings, including those about bodhisattvas.

Mahayana One of the main groups of Buddhists. The name means "the great vehicle."

Mantras Sacred phrases chanted during meditation.

Meditation Sitting quietly and concentrating your mind to achieve inner peace and calm.

Metta Loving kindness. For Buddhists, this is one of the most important qualities a person can have.

Metta Sutta A famous talk given by the Buddha about the importance of metta, or loving kindness.

Nagas Mythical snake-like beings which are half-human and half-god. They are believed to protect the sacred texts until people are ready to receive them.

Nirvana A state of perfect peace and happiness achieved when the fires of hatred, greed, and ignorance are put out.

Noble Eightfold Path One of the key teachings of Buddhism. It shows eight ways for people to lead happy, peaceful lives.

Pali An ancient Indian language, similar to the one spoken by the Buddha. The earliest sacred texts of the Theravada Buddhists were written down in Pali.

Pali Canon The sacred texts of the Theravada Buddhists. Also called the Tipitaka.

Perfect Wisdom A collection of Buddhist texts which teach about Perfect Wisdom, or seeing the truth. This means realizing that nothing lasts forever.

Pirit Verses from the sacred texts which are chanted to protect people from harm.

Prayer wheel A spinning wheel or cylinder which contains Buddhist mantras or prayers written on paper.

Puja The way in which Buddhists practice their religion.

Pure Land A type of Buddhism. Its followers believe in a beautiful, heavenly world, called the Pure Land.

Ratana Sutta A talk given by the Buddha. Also called the Jewel Sutta.

Sangha The Buddhist community.

Sanskrit An ancient Indian language. It was used to write down the first sacred texts of the Mahayana Buddhists.

Siddhattha Gotama The personal, family name of the Indian nobleman who became the Buddha.

Sutta A short, sacred text (in Sanskrit: sutra).

Sutta Pitaka The second of the three collections of texts that make up the Pali Canon. The texts are mostly talks by the Buddha, setting out the key Buddhist teachings.

Tantrayana A type of Buddhism practiced in Tibet that mixes Mahayana and Tantric beliefs.

Tantric A type of Buddhism that uses magic and rituals to help people gain enlightenment. Its name comes from sacred texts called Tantras.

Ten Moral Precepts Ten rules which Buddhist monks and nuns promise to keep. Ordinary Buddhists follow a shorter version, called the Five Moral Precepts.

Tenjur One of the collections of sacred texts of the Tibetan Buddhists.

Theravada One of the groups of Buddhists. The name means "the way of the elders."

Three Jewels The Buddha, the dhamma, and the sangha.

Vihara A Buddhist monastery.

Vinaya The set of rules followed by Buddhist monks and nuns.

Vinaya Pitaka The first of the three collections of texts which make up the Pali Canon. The texts set out the rules of discipline for Buddhist monks and nuns.

Index